How Does Your Garden Grow?

David Keystone

Carole Coburn

Harcourt Achieve

Rigby • Saxon • Steck-Vaughn

www.HarcourtAchieve.com
1.800.531.5015

PM Extensions Nonfiction Emerald Level
How Does Your Garden Grow?
Working with Wood
How Magic Tricks Work
Junk Sculpture
Spin, Weave, Knit, and Knot
The Puppet Show

Rigby PM Extensions
part of the Rigby PM Program
Emerald Level

Published by Harcourt Achieve Inc.
P.O. Box 27010, Austin, Texas 78755.

U.S. edition © 2005 Harcourt Achieve Inc.

First published in 2003 by Thomson Learning Australia
Text © Thomson Learning Australia 2003
Illustrations © Thomson Learning Australia 2003

10 9 8 7 6 5 4 3 2 1
07 06 05 04

Printed in China by 1010 Printing Limited

How Does Your Garden Grow?
ISBN 0 7578 9215 9

Acknowledgements:
The authors and publisher would like to acknowledge permis-
sion to reproduce material from the following sources:
Photographs by Australian Picture Library/ John & Lorraine
Carnemolla, p. 14 bottom; Auscape/ C. Andrew, pp. 13 top left,
13 bottom right, 15/ Kathie Atkinson, pp. 13 top right, 13 bottom
centre/ Wayne Lawler, p. 13 bottom left; Lindsay Edwards, front
cover, back cover, pp. 4, 5, 9, 10-11, 12, 18, 20, 21, 22, 23; Getty
Images/ Stone, p. 13 top centre; Imagen/ Bill Thomas, p. 14 top.

Contents

Chapter 1

1st Month

Introduction

Daniel, Ismini, and Natasha sat eating their lunch outside their classroom. They looked around the yard. It was very bare. There were no shady trees to sit under. Only a few weeds grew here and there.

Mrs. Greene came past them pushing a wheelbarrow. Mrs. Greene was a parent volunteer. She maintained the gardens around the school and taught the students about caring for the environment. She was helping to **landscape** the front of the school. It now had a grassed area and shrubs.

4

As Mrs. Greene pushed the wheelbarrow towards the front gate, Natasha had an idea. "Mrs. Greene said you can make a garden anywhere with the right tools and plants. Perhaps we could make one here at school."

Daniel and Ismini thought this was a fantastic idea.

"My mom made her own garden," said Daniel. "We all helped her."

They talked about Daniel's garden and who did the different tasks to create it. It wasn't very hard if you knew what to do.

They decided to ask Mrs. Greene to help them make a garden on the school grounds.

Design a Garden

Mrs. Greene really liked the students' idea. "Why don't you design the garden yourselves?" she asked them. "Start by planning it on paper. Add the plants you would like and other things, such as paths or rocks."

The students had lots of great ideas for the garden.

Favorite plants
and labels

Animal life —
butterflies, bees, birds

Shade

Nonliving things —
paths, rocks

Flowers
and leaves

Patterns

The students eagerly told Mrs. Greene their ideas. She was impressed! She suggested using a list of these ideas to plan the new garden.

The students made a list of the things they liked most and, with Mrs. Greene's help, they agreed on a design for the garden.

Our garden and what we like

- colorful flowers
- shade
- insects and birds
- places to hide
- curved flower border
- sweet smell of ginger lilies

Chapter 3
1st Month

Tool Shed

"Working in a garden is much easier when you use the correct tools," explained Mrs. Greene, as she opened the shed door. The students stared at the range of tools. "We need to get the soil ready for planting," she said. "I've drawn some tools that we need to use for different jobs. I've written some information about each tool."

Erica's list of tools

spade

a flat blade with a handle for digging and cutting through soil

garden fork

a short handle with teeth to break up the soil and make holes

wheelbarrow

a wheeled vehicle for carrying things easily

rake

a long handle with teeth, for smoothing the soil

hand fork

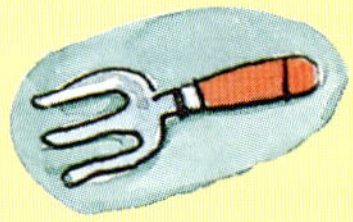

a short handle with teeth for breaking up soil

hand trowel

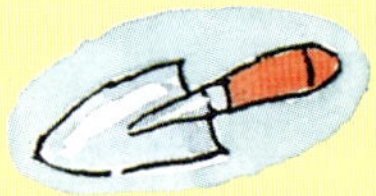

a short handle and blade for making holes for plants

bulb planter

a cylinder with a handle for cutting soil, making holes, and planting bulbs

gloves

worn to protect your hands

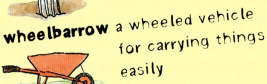

"Will we use all these tools in the garden?" asked Daniel.

"You'll be able to use most of them, but there are some tools that are used only by adults," said Mrs. Greene. "These tools have sharp blades. A lot of care needs to be taken when using them."

Adults Only Tools

Shears garden scissors used for pruning plants

Clippers flat blade garden scissors used for trimming

Preparing the Soil

"Plants need loose, crumbly soil so that their roots can spread easily under the ground," explained Mrs. Greene. "Fine root hairs absorb water and **nutrients** from the loose soil."

Daniel and Natasha used their feet to push the spades and garden forks into the ground. These tools were good levers to break up the soil. Mrs. Greene was busy slicing up weeds with a spade. Ismini helped pile them into the wheelbarrow.

"Weeds can be turned into compost to feed our garden," said Mrs. Greene. "We won't waste anything."

They all worked very hard digging up the ground.

"This soil is sandy. It's easy to dig," said Natasha, resting against her spade.

"Yes," replied Mrs. Greene. "Plants will grow quickly here but the soil will dry out rapidly. We need to make it more spongy."

Nutrients for the Soil

Compost heap

"Compost will help improve our soil," said Mrs. Greene. "Compost is mostly a mixture of plant and vegetable waste. A compost heap breaks down this waste. The waste rots and eventually becomes **humus**. Humus is a good fertilizer for plants."

Natasha dug up the soil lightly. Daniel placed the plastic compost bin over the soil. "Now we will put these weeds in and add some grass clippings," he said.

"Here's a bucket of food scraps we've been collecting in class," said Ismini.

"That's a great idea," said Mrs. Greene. "We need to add waste to our compost every day."

"We make compost at home," said Natasha. "I noticed lots of tiny animals in the humus when Mom was spreading it around her plants."

"Healthy compost is a home for many living things," said Mrs. Greene. "Microscopic living things such as bacteria break it down. They're called micro-organisms. These pictures show some of them. And some bigger creatures help, too."

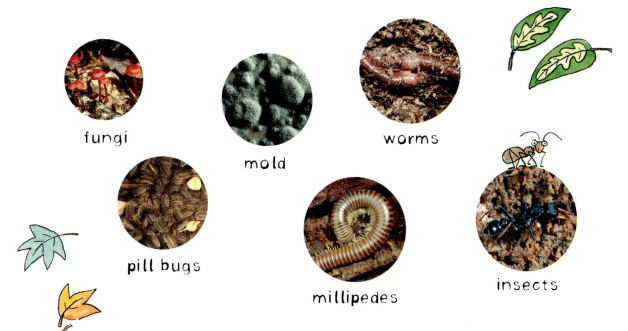

fungi

mold

worms

pill bugs

millipedes

insects

"When we recycle all our scraps we cut down on our waste collection," said Mrs. Greene.

"And it doesn't cost us money to make our compost," added Daniel.

"It helps to improve the soil, too," said Mrs. Greene. "Every gardener knows compost is good for a garden."

Worm farm

"Here's something else that will help our soil," said Mrs. Greene, taking the top off a round box. The students looked in to see hundreds of wriggling worms.

Worm farm

"These are compost worms. They don't live in the soil. We can give them food scraps to eat, which they digest. The worms recycle food we can't eat, such as apple cores and vegetable peel. They will even eat damp shredded paper. The worms' waste makes fertilizer for the garden."

One of the round boxes was sitting on top of the other. The top one, where the worms live, had a lid and drainage holes so that any extra liquid could drain into the bottom box.

"Worms like a cool, moist, and dark **habitat**," said Mrs. Greene. "We need to add a piece of cloth over their food and a daily squirt of water with a spray bottle. The worms will soon be breeding again. Our garden will have rich, spongy soil when we mix in the **worm castings**."

Worm castings

chapter 6

Plants from Plants

Natasha had brought a clump of Iris to school. "Mom said we can divide this plant up into a few smaller plants for our garden," she said.

Iris

"Yes," said Mrs. Greene. "We can make new plants from other plants. We call this plant propagation. We can propagate new plants in many ways. Let me show you how."

Mrs. Greene used a spade to cut the plant into several pieces. "As long as each piece has roots, it will grow," she said. "Plant each piece in a pot with some **potting mix**, and water it well. We'll grow them in pots until we're ready to plant them in the garden."

New plants from cuttings

"We can also take cuttings from different shrubs in the garden," said Mrs. Greene. "We'll take some soft wood cuttings from the green stems. This is how we do it."

Step 1

Cut a stem from a shrub. Each stem needs to have about four leaf nodes. A node is a lump on the stem where a new shoot will grow.

Remove the bottom leaves and cut the stem just below the last node.

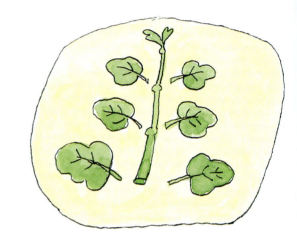

Step 2

Fill a small pot with potting mix. Use a pencil to poke a hole in the mix. Place your cutting in the hole. Label your pot with the name of the plant and the date.

Step 3

Water your cutting immediately. Poke three sticks into the pot to make a frame around the cutting. Cover it with plastic. This keeps the moisture in. Keep the pot out of the sun but in a well lit place. Check the cutting weekly and water it if the soil dries out.

Step 4

Check if your cutting has taken root. Be gentle. If roots have grown, take off the plastic. Let it grow for at least three weeks in the pot. It needs a strong root system to grow in the garden.

Planting Day

When there were many strong roots on the plants, Mrs. Greene knew that the plants were strong enough to survive in the garden. The students were really excited about seeing all the plants in their garden for the first time.

"Let's place the plants where we want them before we plant them," suggested Mrs. Greene. "We'll make certain that they have room to grow."

With the plants laid out in the garden, Mrs. Greene demonstrated how a potted plant is planted in the ground.

How to plant

Step 1

Use a hand trowel to dig a hole wider than the pot.

Step 2

Tap the pot to loosen the root ball and slide the plant out gently.

Step 3

Place the plant in the hole. Check that it is sitting in the soil at the same level as it sat in the pot.

Step 4

Fill the hole with soil. Press the soil firmly and gently around the plant.

Step 5

Generously water the plant immediately.

Planting seeds

Ismini had a packet of poppy flower seeds. They were sealed to keep them fresh. Daniel had a paper bag of seed pods which was splitting and leaking seeds. Mrs. Greene laughed. "I have a tongue twister. Seeds stirred into sifted sand are simple to scatter."

Mrs. Greene mixed the seeds into a bucket of sand and handed it to Daniel.

"You can easily see where the seeds have landed," said Daniel, as he sprinkled the sand and seeds over the bare ground. The students covered the seeds with a fine layer of garden soil.

"We need to keep the soil moist until the seedlings are fairly tall," advised Mrs. Greene.

Planting bulbs

Natasha had some daffodil **bulbs** from her garden.

Bulbs can be divided every year. "They multiply under the ground," said Mrs. Greene. She showed the students how to plant bulbs using a bulb planter. "This tool cuts a hole in the ground. It then removes a plug of soil inside it. Place the bulb, pointy end up, into the hole."

"Now," said Mrs. Greene. "Squeeze the handle on the planter so that the soil falls on top of the bulb."

"I never thought planting bulbs would be so easy," said Daniel.

Caring for the Garden

The group was very eager to observe what happened to their garden.

"After all your hard work," asked Mrs. Greene, "how will you make certain that the garden is well cared for?"

"It's really important to keep the plants in our garden healthy and strong," said Daniel. "I'll make sure we add compost to the garden."

"I'll start a garden diary," said Natasha. "We can write about what works for us and what happens in our garden."

"We could ask others to help water the plants, especially during the school holidays," said Ismini. "We could make a schedule for everyone to follow. Then we would know for sure that our garden will get watered."

"That sounds like a great idea," said Mrs. Greene. "We need to cover the bare soil with **mulch**, too. Putting mulch on the soil will stop it from drying out quickly."

They all spread mulch over most of the garden. The thick carpet of mulch looked much better than the bare ground they had started with.

Then Ismini said, "How about we list all the different jobs? Each of us can choose a job to do. I'll write a name next to each one."

List of gardening jobs

Pruning - Mrs. Greene

Weeding - Daniel

Fertilizing - Natasha

Compost bin - Daniel

Tools - Everyone

Mulching - Mrs. Greene

Worm farm - Ismini

Diary - Natasha

Watering schedule - Ismini

Finished Garden

"Isn't this great?" said Mrs. Greene. "After all our hard work, our garden looks better than we ever imagined."

"I'm sad our garden is finished," said Ismini. "It was so much fun designing and making it. It's starting to look very green, and buds and daisies are starting to appear."

"But Ismini," replied Mrs. Greene, "a garden is never finished. It keeps changing and growing. We can do so much to help it – collect seeds and cuttings from our own plants. We can compost the dead flowers and leaves, and of course we can sit here in the shade and just enjoy it."

> Dear Mrs. Greene, Daniel, Ismini, and Natasha,
>
> We love your new garden. We were wondering if you could help us to design and create a garden, too.
>
> From Mrs. Taylor's third grade class

So Mrs. Greene, Daniel, Ismini, and Natasha did just that!

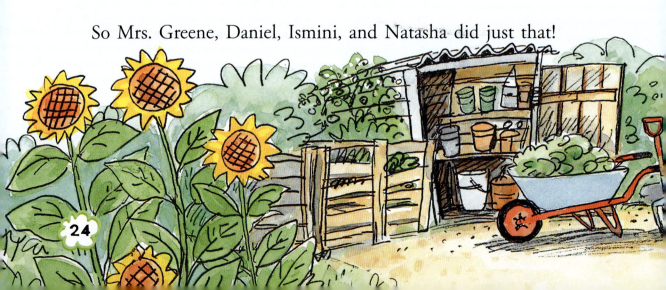